From Storm to Scout

A Little Dog's Big Journey Home

M.V. Despenza

From Storm to Scout

A Little Dog's Big Journey Home

Illustrations by Artmazigh Illustration Team

Interior layout and design by Shahadat Hossain Shahin

ISBN: 979-8-9949161-0-0 (Hardcover)

Published by Books by M.V. Despenza, LLC

Printed in the United States of America

Dedication

For Storm,

who trusted me enough to jump into my truck and begin the journey to your forever home.

I will always hold you in my heart.

Acknowledgements

Thank you to the Artmazigh Illustration Team for your beautiful illustrations, and to Shahadat Hossain Shahin for bringing our story together so wonderfully.

Thank you to Cheryl O'Connor, the kind person who posted the ad, hoping someone would come along and adopt this precious puppy when she could not. Were it not for you, we would never have had the opportunity to spend time with and grow to love this amazing little Schnauzer.

Thank you to Casey and Pam, and to Isabella (yes, you were there), for the time, love, and care you gave to Storm while he was with you.

And a very special thank you to Morris Lott and Johnny Bonfiglio for opening your hearts and your home to Storm—then Scout—and giving him his forever home, where he became your little "Bosco."

The storm roared all night long. Wind howled.
Rain crashed down. And beneath a broken porch,
a little dog waited.

Inside, it was warm and quiet. Miss Vee and her three kitties snuggled close on the couch. Safe and cozy while the storm roared outside.
NEW MESSAGE

Then her phone buzzed. A message flashed across the screen. A little dog was stranded... and he needed a home.

Miss Vee knew the little dog needed help.
So, she went to look for him.

The note said the little dog might bark. But he didn't bark at all. As Miss Vee approached with food, he simply sat and watched her.

As Miss Vee knelt to set the food down, the little dog stepped closer. They looked into each other's eyes. And Miss Vee knew she was taking him home.

Miss Vee began to walk. The little dog walked with her.

She placed him gently on her lap.
He fell fast asleep.

As the kitties peeked in, Miss Vee thought of a name. She smiled. "Storm," she smiled. "I think I'll call you Storm."

Miss Vee gently dried Storm and wrapped him in a warm towel. As she cared for him, something special began to grow between them.

Storm loved his new collar and his bright red bandana. Miss Vee took him for a walk. From the window, three kitties watched quietly. They were not quite sure yet.

Storm followed Miss Vee everywhere. He loved to cuddle and give her kisses. Before long, Miss Vee found herself falling in love with Storm. And Storm loved her right back.

But something had changed. The three kitties missed their special Mommy time with Miss Vee. She saw the way they huddled together and knew they needed her too.

Miss Vee gently stroked Storm's head.
"I love you, Storm," she whispered, "but I need to find you the very best home."
She held him close, wishing she could keep him.

With a heavy heart, Miss Vee made a sign.
She posted it on the board in town.
Storm sat beside her, waiting.

Very soon, Miss Vee got a call. A kind family wanted to meet Storm. She took him over to meet the family. They were very nice. Miss Vee gave Storm one last hug. "I love you," she said softly. "Be my best little boy."

The family was very happy to meet Storm. They knelt
down and scratched behind his ears. "He's perfect,"
they said with big smiles.

But Storm was not alone there. Another dog named Trout lived in the house.
Trout watched Storm carefully. Storm felt unsure.

Trout was not used to sharing. Storm tried to be friendly. But something didn't feel right. Trout was sad, which made his Mommy sad.

They called Miss Vee to come over. They all sat down together. They wanted Storm to have the very best home. And together, they would find him the home he deserved.

They placed an ad in the newspaper. Before long, another family called.
They were looking for a special dog — just like Storm.

They met at the dog park. Storm walked over slowly. A gentle hand reached toward him. Storm wagged his tail.

Storm looked up.
A warm smile met his eyes.
And this time, Storm knew...
the storm was over.

A few weeks later, Storm's new family had a party. Everyone came to see how he was doing. They watched him run and play in his new home.

He had a new home and a new name — Scout.
Scout had finally found his forever family.
And along the way, he found two families who
would always love him.

THE END

Storm's Real Story

(For Bigger Kids & Kids at Heart)

This story was inspired by a real dog
named Storm.

Before he became part of this book,
he was a frightened little dog,
waiting on a porch after the storm.

This is how his journey began.

Two Days after Hurricane Ida.
A kind lady uploaded this post to a
neighborhood app.
The next morning, I responded.

This male dog is wandering around by and hopefully it's owner. will be found it is pitiful I will give it food and water and my neighbor also I could not keep it I have seven dogs

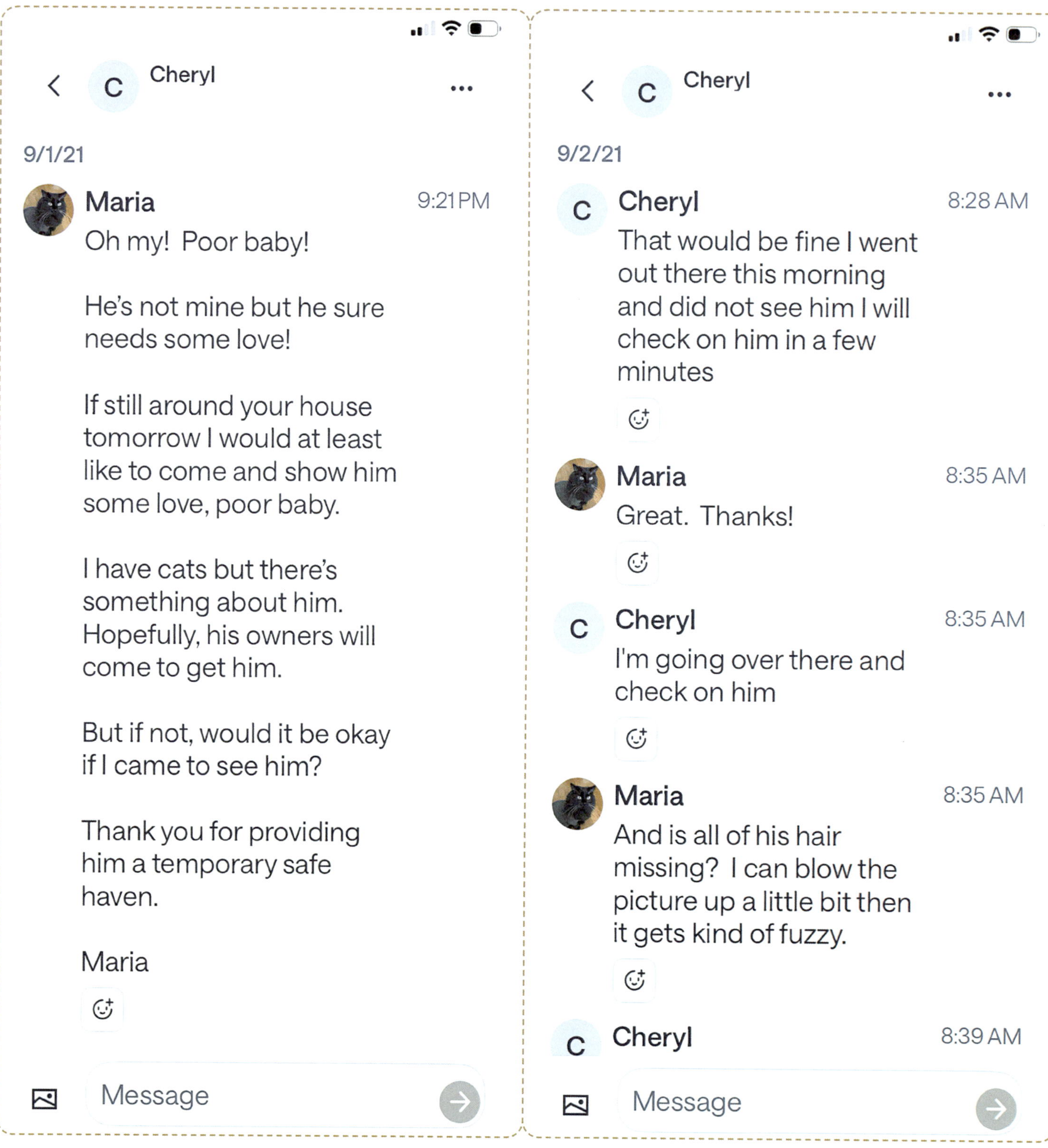
Cheryl
9/1/21
Maria 9:21PM
Oh my! Poor baby!
He's not mine but he sure needs some love!
If still around your house tomorrow I would at least like to come and show him some love, poor baby.
I have cats but there's something about him. Hopefully, his owners will come to get him.
But if not, would it be okay if I came to see him?
Thank you for providing him a temporary safe haven.
Maria
Message
Cheryl
9/2/21
Cheryl 8:28 AM
That would be fine I went out there this morning and did not see him I will check on him in a few minutes
Maria 8:35 AM
Great. Thanks!
Cheryl 8:35 AM
I'm going over there and check on him
Maria 8:35 AM
And is all of his hair missing? I can blow the picture up a little bit then it gets kind of fuzzy.
Cheryl 8:39 AM
Message

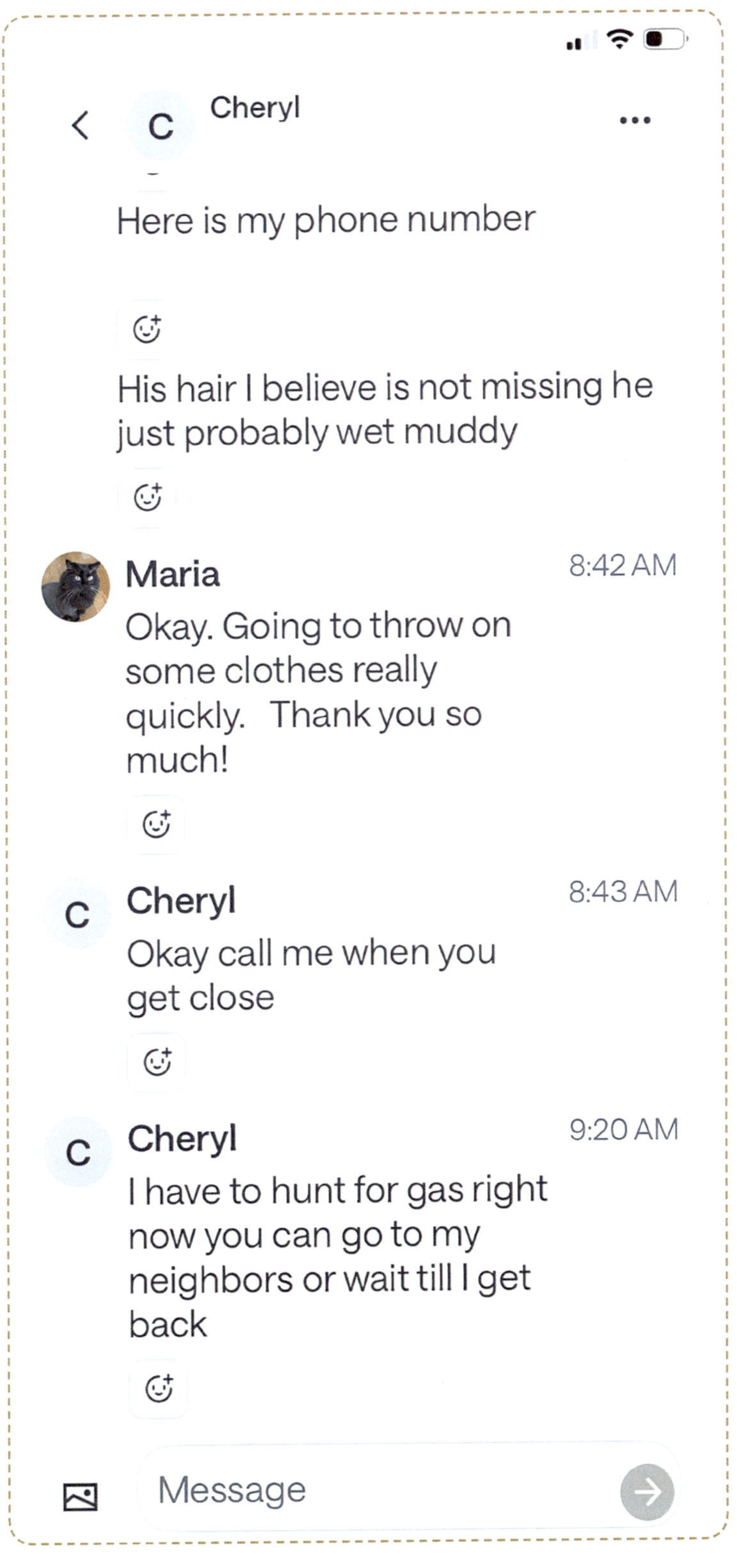
Cheryl
Here is my phone number
His hair I believe is not missing he just probably wet muddy
Maria
8:42 AM
Okay. Going to throw on some clothes really quickly. Thank you so much!
Cheryl
8:43 AM
Okay call me when you get close
Cheryl
9:20 AM
I have to hunt for gas right now you can go to my neighbors or wait till I get back
Message

When I arrived, the little dog did not bark at all.
He just sat there...as if he had been expecting me.

I pulled out a brand-new bag of food from the truck.
I saw that he had food, but there was no bowl.

I wanted to see if he would be aggressive towards me.
But he wasn't.
Not in any way.

His eyes were so sad.
He was so dirty.
As I approached him, his tail began to wag, slowly.

To my left were many workers - saws buzzing,
tree limbs falling.
It was so loud.

I imagine this dog had not slept in over two days.
Fearful of the other strays.
Fearful of the men.
Fearful of the noise.

Maria ...

Desperately Needs a Foster Home Tonight. This precious dog was abandoned or lost. Not sure which. He's an older male, vey healthy (not malnourished at all), SO sweet, and clearly trusting. I brought him home today because he was in an area where larger dogs were astray and the kind lady that told me about him was afraid that they might hurt or kill him. Not sure if his family was forced to evacuate at last minute and couldn't take him or he ran away because of the storm. I do believe his guardians will look for him when they return. But in the interim, I cannot keep him. Have kitty cats inside and don't want to traumatize them.

If you are willing to take him for a week which will give me time to find his owners, I will provide food, a good bath, and $50 for a week's rent if you commit to keeping him inside. I can drop him off before curfew if within a local radius.

In that moment, I knew.
I could not leave him.
He was coming home
with me.
At least until I could find
his owners or...
find him a new home.

No one ever claimed him.
I put up signs.
He was not microchipped.
In the aftermath of the storm,
no one was in a position to foster a little doggie.
So, I decided to do it myself.

And the frightened little dog on the porch...
became Storm.

A Note About Rescue Animals

Storm's story was inspired by a real moment when a frightened little dog trusted a stranger enough to jump into a truck and begin the journey to a forever home.

Many animals are still waiting in shelters or being cared for by rescue groups, hoping someone will see them and give them the love they deserve.

Sometimes we think we are choosing them. But the truth is, they're choosing us. I cannot think of a greater honor.

M. V. Despenza

If you are thinking about bringing a pet into your life, please consider adopting from a rescue or shelter.

About the Author

M. V. Despenza lives in Louisiana and believes that some of life's most meaningful stories begin in the most unexpected ways. She writes about love, connection, and the unforgettable bond between people and the animals who become family and change our lives for the better.

Bonus
Coloring Pages

Scout

www.ingramcontent.com/pod-product-compliance
Ingram Content Group UK Ltd.
Pitfield, Milton Keynes, MK11 3LW, UK
UKRC032027290726
14090UKWH00008B/485